First published in 2005 by Conari Press,
an imprint of Red Wheel/Weiser, LLC
York Beach, ME
With offices at:
368 Congress Street
Boston, MA 02210
www.redwheelweiser.com

ISBN 1-57324-258-6

Typeset in Shmelvetica by Kathleen Wilson Fivel
Printed in China
Everbest
12 11 10 09 08 07 06 05
8 7 6 5 4 3 2 1

Ask Gladys

Household Hints for Gals on the Go

Enjoy!
Phyllis Root

Photos by Kelly Povo
Words by Phyllis Root & Kelly Povo

Kelly Povo
2005

CONARI PRESS

Flunked another white glove test?

Can't keep on top
of your laundry?

Sick of housework?

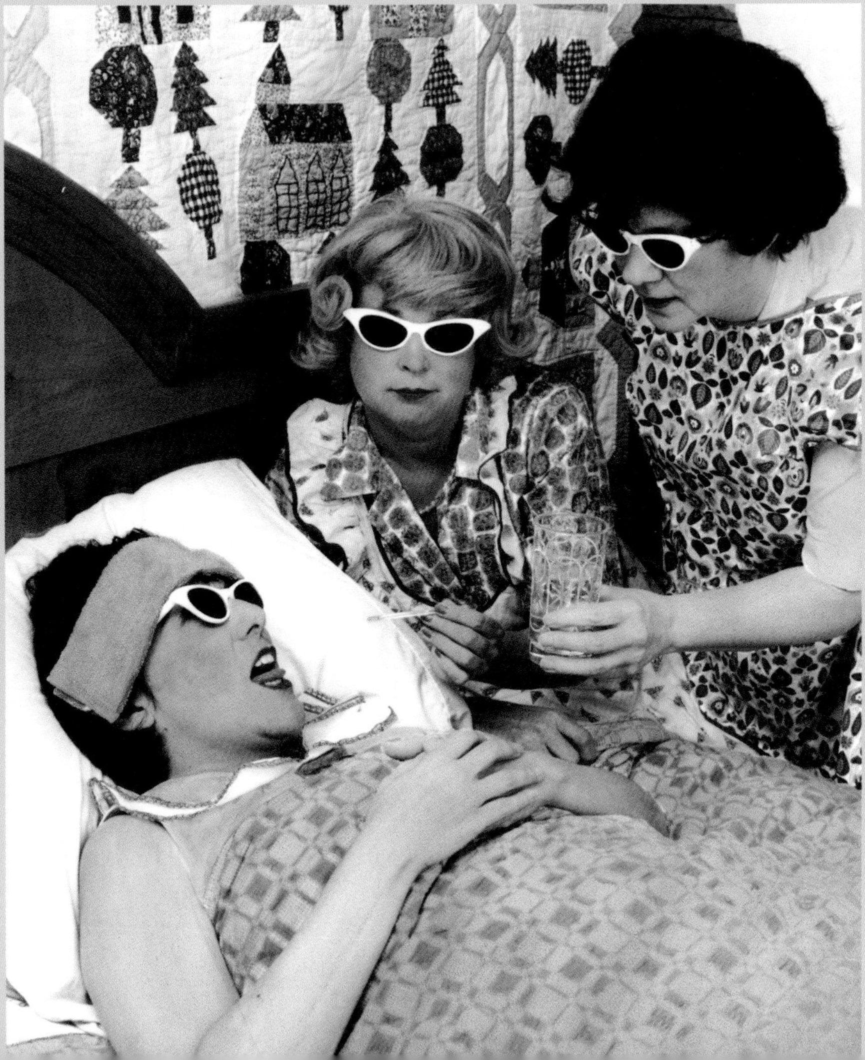

Ask Gladys!

She'll show you
how to bust that dust,

drop that mop,

and still have time
to smell the flowers.

Help! Clutter is popping up everywhere! What can I do?

Gladys promises,
You can polish off that mess
and make your house shine!

Keep someone in bed
so you never have to make it.

GLADYS!
Honey-Do List
How to keep her
Not a lock in sight...new
SILHOUETTE by Samsonite
Samsonite
Silhouette

Delegate

Multitask.

Save time—
shower with your dishes.

Yikes!
People laugh at my cooking.
Make them stop!

Gladys declares,
It's not burnt, it's Cajun!

Dazzle your guests.

Serve food they can relish.

Make every meal a party.

Happy
Birthday

And always make the gravy
before the second martini!

Aaargh!
I can't face another day
of housework!
Save me!

Gladys advises,
Practice a calm frame of mind.

Harmonize
with your housework.

Be the dust bunny.

CAUTION

Don’t be afraid
to tackle the hard jobs.

If all else fails, downsize.

Downsize more.

Move.

Whatever you do,
do it with flair.

Do it with style.

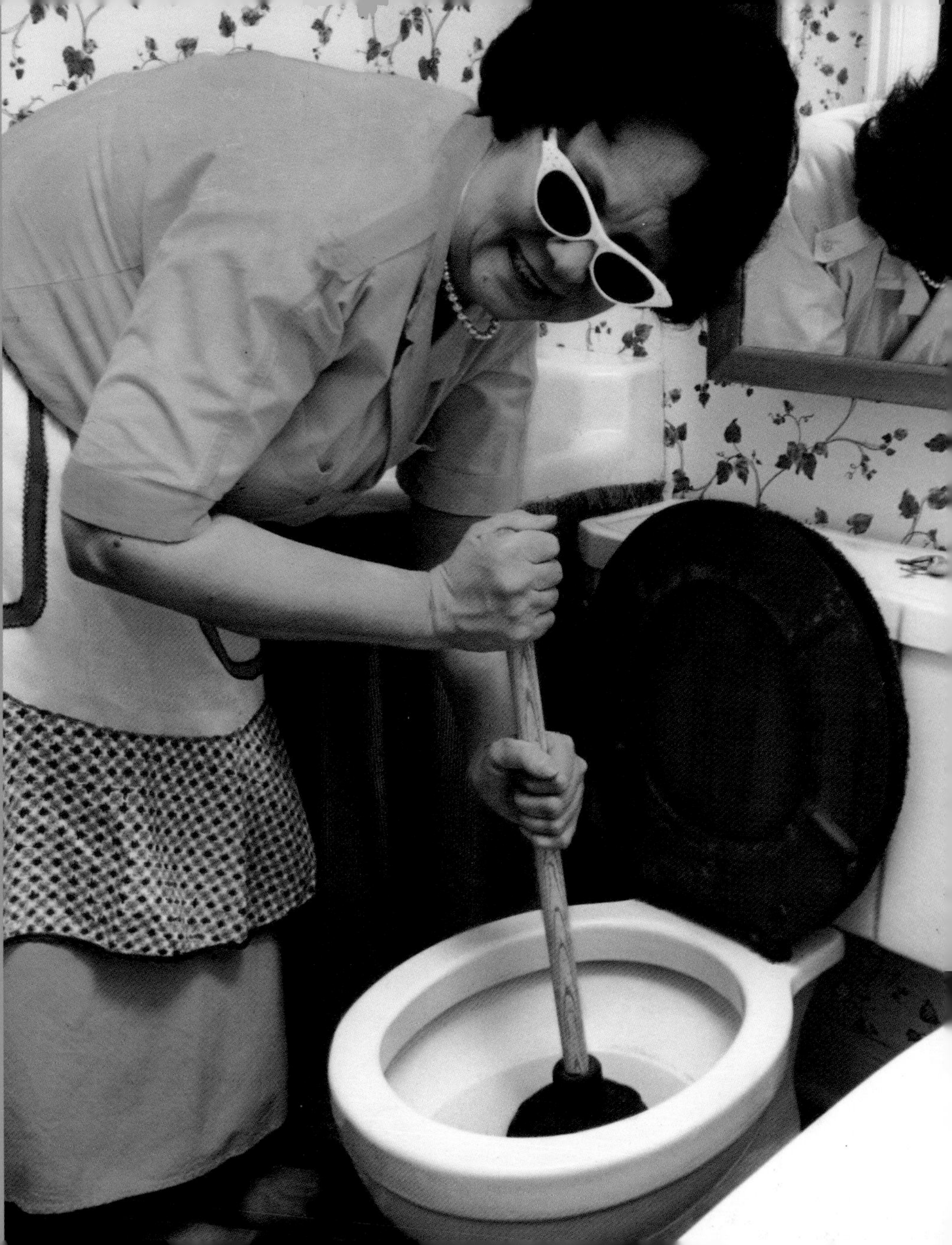

Do it with Gladys!

Always remember—
you're stronger than dirt.

CAT
ZIEGLER CAT

You can handle anything!

No question about it!

When not on the go, Kelly Povo and Phyllis Root always make sure to keep their homes spotless. They have been friends for many years and spend most of their time together laughing, even though they don't always remember what was so funny. Kelly and Phyllis also collaborated on Hot Flash Gal and Gladys on the Go. Kelly has her own greeting card line (visit her at www.kellycards.com) and Phyllis writes children's books.